An
entirely new way
of explaining
plant names

This book provides a set of clues

... 'Pansies are
for thoughts' as we
all know ...

First published 1996
Ety Publications, New Zealand

© 1996 text: Fay Clayton
Illustrations: Phillip Hart
All rights reserved

Re-printed 1998
Pentland Press Ltd.
1 Hutton Close
South Church
Bishop Auckland
Co. Durham

ISBN 1 85821 556 0

Botanical Editors: Raymond Mole and John Dawson
Script Editor: Lisa Ritchie

Desktop production by Wordset Enterprises Limited
This edition printed by Lintons Printers, Co. Durham, England.

Handbook
for the
Baffled Gardener!
What those plant names mean

Fay Clayton

Dedicated to my parents
from whom I learned a love of gardening

This book, the third in a trilogy, selects the generic names of house and garden ornamentals where those names recall no people – men or women – and no deities. It's about other names.

Selection has been necessary. Some plants are better known than others; some are more greatly loved; and some quite ordinary plants have names that are crammed with interest. We have tried to balance these three aspects. Plants are given either a short description or a full narrative; and in the last chapter they are merely annotated. Those last plants, however, are still an integral part of this text.

There is a saying in our language – "It's all Greek to me!" That means "Don't talk to me of that! I don't understand a word". The fact is that Greek is firmly embedded in our language – as is Latin. If we can unbed them, meet them face to face in words familiar to us, then we recognise them easily in those often daunting plant names … and surprises pop up, one by one.

Illustrated by Phillip Hart

Contents

Foreword

Garden lovers are students for life. For garden lovers of all ages this little book completes Fay Clayton's trilogy on the romance that can be found in the naming of plants. She is not only an intriguing researcher of botanical nomenclature but she is a compelling teacher. One reads "Nigella, love-in-a-mist ... is a popular garden plant, a love-blue flower, veiled in its own green mist ... so why nigella? ... It is named from *niger*, Latin, black ... within the seed-pod can be found seeds that are black indeed and very small. ... Nigella is a good name for the keen botanist or observant gardener." These word pictures permeate the book and lead the reader on through a peaceful process of learning. One is continually saying to oneself, "So that is how it got its name," and the name remains and the student has learned. That is what Fay Clayton's captivating and very educational little books on the derivation of generic plant names are all about. As with *Gentlemen in my Garden* and *Deities in my Garden* Phillip Hart's illustrations add dignity to the pages. All her books will sit with pride on any library shelf.

J. O. Taylor MBE
President
Royal New Zealand Institute of Horticulture

Botanical Editors' Notes

What's in a name? For discerning gardeners and aspiring amateur botanists – one may learn a great deal.

This publication is the third in a trilogy which seeks to highlight the meaning of selected generic plant names. These plants have features which, in some way, are akin to various entities such as body parts of creatures, colour and shapes.

Many hours of painstaking research into the interpretation of word meanings and their adaptation of Greek and Latin words by astute botanists have been carried out by the author who has tackled a subject rarely seen in such a comprehensive form. Readers should find the information useful and fascinating.

Raymond H Mole
Horticultural and Botanical Consultant

Sadly, Ray Mole's death, after a long illness, prevented him from completing the botanical editing of this book. As his friend and colleague I have been happy to complete the task.

In this work generic names only have been considered, although popular names, where they exist, have also been provided. Unfortunately generic names sometimes change or disappear in the light of botanical research. For instance, it is sometimes considered that two genera are not sufficiently different to be kept apart, so they are combined under one name.

The number of species in a genus can also change for the same reasons, or by the discovery of new species. The *Royal Horticultural Society Dictionary* 1992 has been the source for currently accepted generic names and their number of species.

John Dawson
Botanical Consultant

Introduction –
the element of surprise

A list of generic names can be baffling, to
say the least. Faced with the prospect of
sorting them out in my own mind, one
initial surprise for me was to discover just how
many plants are named after men – and I found I
was not alone. There are words so softly feminine –
camellia, magnolia (pictured) and allamanda – and
what have you got – a priest, a professor and a physician.
Some folk practically swoon over the dew-drop beauty and
porcelaine perfection of hoya – and there you have an
English gardener, Tom Hoy . . . hence *Gentlemen in my Garden*.

The surprise element evaporates in the light of history, for,
though plants had earlier been named after men, it was Father Charles
Plumier, sent three times to the Americas by his king, Louis XIV, who
named fifty plants in this way, including begonia, fuchsia and lobelia.
After his death the practice continued. Such names are legion.

The next surprise for me was this: plants the Greeks would never
have known are named after their gods and goddesses. Hemerocallis,
day beauty, of east China and Japan, rings in the glory of *Hemera*,
goddess of the day. Helianthus, sunflower, of America, fairly shouts
the praises of *Helios*, sun god. Protea of South Africa, does honour to
that protean god of the sea, *Proteus*, able to assume so many shapes.
Hebe, completely southern with homelands mainly in New Zealand,
raises its little cup-flowers in honour of *Hebe*, goddess of youth and
cupbearer to the gods. These surprises too evaporate when we see the
reasoning: it's the modern mind reaching back to the Greeks, for
imagery and metaphor – hence *Deities in my Garden*.

Another way of naming plants is from the language of their place
of origin. This is most likely with Old World plants. Let's now go to the
east and find plants native there and not elsewhere. We have gingko
from ancient Chinese, jasminum from Persian, tulipa from Turkish,
luculia from Nepalese, kalanchoe from Mandarin, and aucuba and
nandina both from Japanese. Then suddenly we come across

paulownia and gardenia, both native to China, but named respectively after a Russian Princess, Anna Paulovna (1795–1865) and a physician of South Carolina, Alexander Garden (1730–1791). Surprises continue.

Once we search out meanings of Latin or Greek surprises never cease. A name may be a song of praise – aster is compared to a star, phlox is likened to a flame, and diosma is the scent of the gods, no less. A name may be merely a description or comparison – gladiolus is like a sword, campanula like a bell. Some names reflect human characteristics as if plants can get impatient, mimic, race to be first, be strong, inclined to sit, run over the heath, play at being monsters or dress in shining apparel giving us impatiens, mimosa, primula,crataegus, sedum, hypericum, monstera and photinia.

Names can also be insults. Astilbe is accused of having no glitter, and coreopsis of having seeds like bedbugs! The plants, of course, neither blush nor look proud. They speak no Latin or Greek.

The attributes of one species often give rise to the name of the whole genus, but you can have a little giggle when you realise that *your* scabiosa will not cure scabies; *your* alyssum will not cure rabies! and *your* mimosa will not mimic fear. You can merely note that there is a reason for the name.

Reference is often made to colour or shape, likeness to an animal or body part; or to a special characteristic. Here the eternal surprise is the *part* of the plant inspiring the name. It may be the leaf, seed, stamen, corm or rhizome, or the flower shape.

Three samples follow: cyclamen tosses its shuttlecock head in the air in a most engaging way, but is named for its cyclical or rounded corm … not fair really, with all that beauty above ground. Myosotis with its drift of baby blue is named for its quite ordinary leaf. Pick one. Close your eyes and feel it, soft, small, furry and pointed. Can you feel a mouse, *myos*; ear *otis* … you've probably never held a mouse so closely … you wouldn't know. Have another feel. Aquilegia, so delicately beribboned, so pastel-shaded and graceful, is likened to the eagle, *aquila*, from Latin.

Like eagles we want to fly high – to get a bird's eye view of generic names. For ease of identification plants here have been divided into fields of thought. These appear as chapter headings. Creatures will leap for you, like the dolphin, an arrow of blue you see in your delphinium. Horsemen will ride for you in hippeastrum. The gentle donkey will wiggle appreciative nostrils at onosma. You'll find yourself peering into flower heads and seed-pods, examining roots and leaves and stamens.

Objects and bodily parts, and ideas both trivial and noble will present themselves to you as you make your way through the book. In this pursuit I have been informed, bemused, delighted, and had many a quiet chuckle at full discovery of the meaning and reason for a name. May your garden – even the smallest of gardens – become as a miniature museum reflecting the activities and interest of humanity.

This work is about words as much as it is about plants. The origin of a plant name is taken from its earliest source. When the origin is not supplied, assume that word is from Greek, as it so often is. Sometimes it reads better without stating 'Greek' all the while. Where it is suitable Latin or Greek words or part words are given their English form. The century during which a word became part of our written language is supplied where it is known, thus: (c16) i.e. in the sixteenth century. This simple addition throws light on the history of the name and adds to our appreciation.

The name Linnaeus (1707–1778) occurs frequently. He was the first to formalise the botanic naming of plants. Where it is known that he either sanctioned the use of an earlier name or coined a new name that is noted thus: (Linnaeus).

Family names are supplied for botanical exactitude and to indicate relationships; where appropriate, the species name is also given; for the most part no attempt is made to explain these. That is beyond the confines of this book.

Handbook
for the
Baffled Gardener
What those plant names mean

*Down the garden path we go
in search of names of plants ...*

Rose and Rhododendron Lead the Way

Rosa "Rose" *Rosacea* 100–150 species   This genus has been hybridised over thousands of years, with more resultant forms and variety in colour than any other plant

… and what could be more English! From 1629 it was England's foremost emblem used in heraldry and decoration … but its name is from Latin, *rosa*, rose. Roses are northern, for the most part growing naturally in that hemisphere only. The earliest English would have known the rose, but, left to themselves would possibly still be calling it the sweet brier. Symbol of love this might well be the most loved flower in all the world.

It is thought that *rosa* is related to the Greek word for rose – *rhodon* …

Rhododendron "Azalea" "Vireya" *Ericaceae* 700–800 species.
Rhododendron means rose tree. It's a Greek word but was adopted by the Roman writer, Pliny (c.23–79 AD) to name the oleander. All that was so long ago.

In the seventeenth century – 1656 to be exact – some massive and beautiful shrubs were brought into England for the first time. These were plants of the mountains, thriving at altitudes of thousands of metres, and people in England viewing them for the first time were inspired by those great trusses of red flowers. The big question was what to call them. Rhododendron was chosen – rose tree, an apt name full of imagery for this spectacular plant, one of the most important ornamentals in our gardens. Their homelands include the Himalayas and the mountainous regions of China, Europe and America.

There is much to choose from in this genus which ranges in height from ground-hugging forms of up to ten centimetres only, through to massive trees some twenty-five metres tall. Moreover there are over nine thousand named hybrids. No wonder 'rhodos' are so special in our gardens.

Azalea is a sub-group. In 1753 Linnaeus chose this name, which means dry, a reference to its preferred habitat. Azaleas are dwarf, small-leafed, and may be deciduous or evergreen.

Vireya, a huge sub-group, comprises about a third of the total number of species. They are evergreen shrubs and small trees, and their homelands are tropical areas of south-east Asia. They are very special: their little winged seeds must find a place and germinate within a few weeks or they perish.

Julian Vireya, a seventeenth century Frenchman had his own trade, but did such good work as an amateur botanist that this section of rhododendrons is named after him.

We walk in the dappled shade of our own private gardens, but our thoughts can rise to lofty homelands.

Rose is from Latin, rhododendron from Greek. They lead the way. Let's follow ...

Flower

(Anthus, Anthemum)

Blossom, a word familiar to us all, was the Old English word for flower, but from the thirteenth century it came to be used of massed blooms only, replaced in the language by flower, from French *fleur*. This was a natural consequence of history. It is often forgotten that the French ruled England for three centuries. Then in the fourteenth century, with troubles at home, they departed, but their marvellous language remained, and so we have flora, florist, florid, inflorescence. … The final source though is Latin, *flos*, *floris* and *Flora*, Roman goddess of flowers.

When it comes to giving plants generic names, however, we turn to the Greek word for flower, *anthos* – a word ringing in true beauty, for it has an ancestor in Sanskrit meaning maiden. Untouched beauty, pristine perfection is found in flowers. If it comes to that, our own use of *anth* – is equally poetic in the word anthology, an *-ology* or collection of the 'flowers of thought' of poets!

Now to botany. In the original Greek there are two forms of the word – *anthos* and *anthemon*, which, Latinised become *anthus* and *anthemum*. Generic names using anth- are legion. We do not seek the exotic here, for in your garden and in mine many can easily be found. Dianthus, flower of the deity and helianthus, sunflower appear in *Deities in my Garden*. In the following pages we will meet chrysanthemum, gold flower; cyanthus, blue flower; amaranthus, unfading flower; cheiranthus, hand flower; and haemanthus, blood flower; but many more can be found. Here we have a selection.

Clianthus "Glory pea" "Parrot's bill" *Leguminosae* 2 species. It's great to start with glory. That's what this name means – the glory flower. C. *speciosa* of Australia is called the glory pea. C. *puniceus* of New Zealand is the kaka beak, *kaka* being Maori for parrot.

Lisianthus *Gentianaceae* 27 species.   How critical! This flower has wobbly habits in the garden or in vase – and so is named uncertain flower!

Aeschyanthus *Gesneriaceae* 100 species.   If we admire shy or modest habits, then this is our flower, its name from a verb, to be ashamed, from its modest habit of bearing its flowers.

Mesembryanthemum *Aizoaceae* 40–50 species.   This is a ridiculously long name for a flower that is in itself so simple, so daisy-like. Seize upon that *mes-* the middle, in this case the middle of the day. Closing in the dark or shade, opening in light, this is the noon-flower, best in the heat of the day.

Chimonanthus "Wintersweet" *Calycanthaceae* 6 species.   We think of time again and call this cheimonanthus, the winter flower, thus acknowledging *cheimon*, Greek winter. And we love it for its timing.

Cyrtanthus *Amaryllidaceae* 47 species.   The flowers curve down from the apex of the scape, so we call this the curved flower. Our word curve comes from the Greek *cyrt-* and circle and circus are related words.

Melianthus "Honey flower" *Melianthaceae* 6 species.   Because the tubes contain a wealth of nectar this is the honey flower, from *mel*, honey, familiar to us in mellifluous, flowing like honey.

Osmanthus "Fragrant olive" *Oleaceae* 30 species.   Plainly this is the scented flower from Greek *osmē*, smell.

Plectranthus *Labiatae* 350 species.   Have look at the hard spur on a cock's leg, *plectron*, or just imagine it as you observe the flowers on your plant – probably spreading marvellously beneath the trees.

Schizanthus "Butterfly flower" *Solanaceae* 12 species.   No courtesy here. This is the split flower, its little face seeming split in two. Butterfly flower suits it. *Schiz-* we find in schizophrenia.

Galanthus "Snowdrop" *Amaryllidaceae* c.14 species.   The snowdrop pops up early, sometimes before winter snows have dispersed. It's a humble flower, its head drooping. If only one night it could look up and see its word-mate in the sky – the Galaxy, the Milky Way. Both Galaxy and galanthus come from *gala, galactos*, milk.

Anthurium *Araceae* 700–900 species.   Let's finish with a tail-piece – and a bit of cheek! This is the flower with a tail! *oura*, used as *ur-* … a humorous name for a flower with a lovely spadix in a spathe.

Agapanthus

Flower of agape,
Flower of hospitality,
Flower of the highest form
of love.

Agapanthus *"African Lily"* *Liliaceae* c.10 species. Pride of place in this chapter must surely go to agapanthus – despised by many – but so faithful, asking so little for itself. This is the love-flower – which must be explained, for in English we use the word love too lightly.

The Greeks divided love into four: *storge*, the natural love of parent for offspring; *eros*, that erotic feeling we have for a mate or possible mate, which we all experience with varying rates of success; and *philos*, best translated as friendship or liking-for. This last is discussed more fully under Philodendron in the chapter Tree, page 11.

The highest form of love is *agape* (pronounced in three syllables), defined in most dictionaries as that love feast held by the early Christians at communion time when contributions were made for the poor. Agape means Christian love, selfless love, unconditional love – often shown by saints and philanthropists – Francis of Assisi, Mother Teresa of Calcutta – or the late Fred Hollows – helping those for whom, often, there could be no natural attraction whatever. This is a useful concept for anyone. We may have, temporarily, not a trace of love for our offspring. For our mate we may have, temporarily no *eros*, or *philos* or liking either, but in each case we still continue to do the sorts of things we ought to do, because of our commitment. Splendid! Our other loves return.

And so to our flower. There are about ten species, though classification is confused. Native to Africa and of the lily family African lily is accurate enough, but agapanthus it is, flower of hospitality. It's easy to grow in almost any soil. I have shifted it in full flower from one place to another to suit a special occasion, and the high flowering stems went right on flowering, no bending of the stalk, no sulking – no desertion of duty. For my part, I feel we'd have been better off if the -e- had stayed. We'd have had to say agape/anthus. (C19)

A note on anther: Early medicines often consisted of the internal organs of flowers, referred to by pharmacists as anthera, the 'flower part of the flower'. Later herbalists used anther (new spelling) only of that part of the stamen that contains the pollen. This use was sanctioned by Linnaeus.

Seed

(Spermum, Sporum)

The English word seed is used first of the seed of plants and also of the seed of men and animals. For the Romans it was the same: their word *semen*, primarily used of plants, also meant seed of men and animals. Used figuratively it meant origin or source – and even today we have seminars where seeds of thought are sown. It's the Greek *sperma* we use in botany. All plants are divided into angiosperms, with seed in *angeion*, a vessel, and gymnosperms, with seed *gymnos*, naked, not in a vessel or closed ovary. Selected plants follow.

Leucospermum *Proteaceae*   46 species. Known to Europeans only recently, its very Greek name means white seed. For *leuc-* white, see the chapter Colour, page 14. Examine the seeds yourself.

Osteospermum *Asteraceae*   c.70 species. The daisy-like flowers on these perennials or shrubs have striking colouring, but the bone-like seeds inspire osteospermum, from *osteo-* bone. Now meet our special guest.

Leptospermum "Manuka" "Tea tree" "Ti-tree" *Myrtaceae* 79 species.   Most species of leptospermum are native to Australia though some belong to New Zealand. Manuka is the Maori name. Early settlers used the tiny leaves for tea – hence tea tree. When flowering is over there is left a small hard sort of nut – hardly slender! If you are a person with a small bodily frame you are a leptosome. *Lepto-* is used in various scientifice terms where slenderness is a feature. So, see on the nut or cone the thin slits through which the thin seeds slip – in due time. If you can't wait, take a small hammer and crack open the nut. Thinness is the main feature of these seeds.

When we sow seed we scatter it. The Greeks had a word – *spora* – for seed or a scattering, a sowing. From this we have our word sporadic. Spore is now added to our vocabulary. (C19) We use -*sporum* as an ending when it serves a purpose. Plant names follow.

Hymenosporum "Australian frangipani" *Pittosporaceae* 1 species. This is an outstandingly beautiful tree, endemic to Australia, interesting for its name from *hymen*, membrane, and *sporum*, seed. The seed has a membranous wing.

Pittosporum *Pittosporaceae* c.200 species. Pittosporum is a genus of evergreen trees and shrubs popular as leafy fillers. They are mostly native to Australasia – very common in New Zealand – though some species come from China and Japan. One species, P. *crassifolium*, with its leathery leaves, dark green above and white or russet and velvety below, is now popular for hedges in Cornwall and in the Scilly Isles. Among the approximately two hundred species there is variation in shape, size and colour of leaves, but the flowers can all fairly be described as shortly tubular or bell-shaped, with reflexed petals.

They are named, however, for their seed. Pitch is a sticky resinous black or dark brown substance, obtained by distilling tar. It has long been used for caulking the seams of ships. The word pitch is very old and found in various forms in many languages. Open up the seed-pod and see if you think pitchy-seed is a good name: the ending -*sporum* is used because the seed can certainly be scattered far, when it sticks to the feet of birds.

Tree
(Dendron, Dendrum)

The word tree from Old English is known to us from early childhood, but early too we learn the Latin *arbor*, from Arbor days when we plant trees. In arboretums we grow trees. Our arboreal friends, the monkeys, live in trees, and an arborescence is a tree-like formation.

The Greek *dendron*, tree, we use much more. For example, the study of trees is dendrology; and if it includes the element of *chronos*, time, with the counting of rings, it is dendrochronology. A dendrite is a crystalline formation in the shape of a tree, found in rocks. ... No surprise therefore when, in plant nomenclature we find *dendr-* as part of the name of a genus. Rhododendron, rose tree, we've already met on page 3. Other plants follow.

Liriodendron "Tulip tree" *Magnoliaceae* 2 species. After about fifteen years of growth these trees bear tulip-shaped flowers, hence tulip tree; but the botanical name translates as lily tree, from Greek *leirion*, lily. Confounded by the beauty, perhaps we've mixed our metaphors – lily/tulip!

Clerodendron *Verbenaceae* 400 species. This means chance tree with reference to the variable medical properties of some species. Take your chance and you just might get better.

Epidendrum *Orchidaceae* 500 species. This is *epi-* upon, *-dendrum*, a tree. Most species are epiphytic, though some are lithophytic, that is they grow over stone.

Dendrobium *Orchidaceae* 900–1400 species. Like the above, this genus has lithophytic species, but by far the greatest number are epiphytic. Indeed this is one of the largest genera of orchids growing on trees. Moreoever, there is wide variation in size and form, and some with rod-like stems bearing hundreds of flowers could indeed be mistaken for trees.

Other genera ending *-dendron*, or *-dendrum* can be found, a sampling only here. Now pride of place must be given to philodendron which is not a tree at all!

Philodendron *Araceae* 350 species.   Many a home-owner or office worker will know the philodendron, a splendid easy care house plant, one of the treasures we have from tropical America. There are three hundred and fifty species in the genus, most vigorous climbers; one of these, frequently cultivated, is P. *scandens*, literally the climbing one. Consider it: it produces aerial roots at every node, and in its natural state climbs trees, clinging to them, seemingly very fond of them. We are all familiar with the Greek *philos*, friendship or liking: the philharmonic orchestra likes harmony; the philosopher likes *sophos*, wisdom; the philodendron likes trees. And there's more: a typical feature of most species, whether climbing or not, is that the young leaves often come in the shape of a heart. Philodendron is a good name.

Leaf
(Folium, Phyllum)

Leaf, Old English, is a word we use for the leaves of a tree and the leaves of a book. We do the same with the Latin word *folium*, for we have foliage and folios. A person with a portfolio carries leaves – whole bags of them!

The Greek word is *phyllum*. These two words *folium* and *phyllum* are thought to be related. It's not certain, but they sound alike and linking them makes *phyllum*, leaf, easier to remember. A selection of plant names follows.

Trifolium "Clover" "Shamrock" *Leguminosae* c.230 species. Perhaps we know this best as farm fodder – or a pest in the lawn – but there are garden species. Plainly this is three-leaf – unless you find a four-leaf clover!

Epiphyllum *Cactaceae* c.15 species. These cacti produce large, showy, bell-shaped flowers which may be as much as fourteen centimetres across. They appear on what seem to be leaves, hence the name *epi-* upon and *-phyllum* leaf. A misnomer. Those leaves are in fact stems. Interesting when you examine the plant.

Stamen
(Stemon)

The warp of a loom, the long thread, the Romans called *stamen*, and when Pliny (c.23–79) was searching round for botanical language he chose this to name the upright filaments in the lily. We've adopted it (C17) and use it more generally. The earlier source is Greek *stemon*. A plant selection follows.

Callistemon "Bottle brush" *Myrtaceae* 25 species. The practical new settlers called this Australian genus bottle brush, but those filaments or stamens are beautiful – hence callistemon, beautiful stamen. For *calli-* beautiful see the chapter Beauty, page 17.

Penstemon *Scrophulariaecea* c.250 species. We are familiar with *pente*, five, in Pentagon, that building in Arlington with five angles and therefore five sides. Penstemon is not so much five stamens but fifth stamen, which is predominant and sterile!

Fruit
(Carpus)

The English named fruit native to their land – apple, blackberry … but did not have a general term. Fruit comes from Latin *fructus*, enjoyment! The Greek *karpos*, alternative spelling, carpus, we use in plant genera. For instance the breadfruit tree is botanically A*rtocarpus*, from *artos*, bread and *carpus*, fruit. The fruit, roasted, resembles bread and is an important food in the South Sea Islands where it is native. During an expedition to collect this plant the mutiny on the *Bounty* occurred. Now we consider a garden selection.

Callicarpa "Beauty-berry" *Verbenaceae* c. 140 species. These deciduous shrubs and small trees – mostly tropical – are grown for the beauty of their clusters of lilac berries in autumn – perfectly named beautiful fruit. For *calli-* see the chapter Beauty, page 17.

Streptocarpus "Cape primrose" *Gesneriaceae* c.130 species. This is a charming genus with flowers often foxglove shape, but the name comes because of the fruit. In Greek twisted is *strepto-* familiar to us in streptococcus, bothering us in scarlet fever. Here we must look at the long seed pod, twisted.

Podocarpus "Podocarp" "Yellow-wood" *Podocarpaceae* c.100 species. Let's just touch upon the podocarps, great forest trees, grown across the world, named for the foot or stalk (pod) at the fleshy base of the fruit. For *pod*, foot, see the chapter Body Parts, page 38. There's one I'd never be without – *Podocarpus totara*, the golden variety, bringing sunny colour into the garden. Slow growing and easily pruned to shape it is a wonderful ornamental.

Thorn
(Acanthus)

Acanthus "Bear's breeches" *Acanthaceae*. 30 species. *Acantha* is Greek for thorn – almost as if the language were trying to say *ac-*sharp, *anthus*, bloom. Some species have thorns. These handsome herbaceous perennials were the inspiration for the decoration of Corinthian columns. Bear's breeches is picturesque. For Pyracantha, firethorn, see page 32.

Scent

(Osma)

Everybody loves a scented garden, yet the quality of smell enters into few generic names. The Greek word for smell is *osmē*. Osmanthus, scented flower, can be found in the chapter Flower, page 5. Onosma, the smell that asses love, can be found in the chapter Creatures, page 27. Two further samples follow.

Coprosma *Rubiaceae* c.90 species.   These Australasian shrubs, sometimes used as ornamentals are given a very Greek name – but not a complimentary one. From *kopros*, dung and *osmē*, smell, scent of dung arises because many of the plants are foetid when bruised.

Diosma "Breath of Heaven" *Rutaceae* c.28 species.   Greeks would never have seen this South African shrub, named so superbly in Greek – scent of the gods, scent of the deities; divine smell, if you like.

Colour

Colour is predominant in the garden – not so easy to find in generic names, but it is there in Latin or Greek, red, white, blue, gold, violet, green and black. Selected plant names follow.

Rhus "Sumach" *Grossulariaceae* c.200 species. Rhus joins many of our words beginning r- where redness is implied. In this genus red is predominant, R. *glabra* a great sample, leaves turning brilliant red in autumn and the fruit even deeper red.

Leucadendron *Proteaceae* c.80 species. Unhappily we are all too familiar with *leuk-* white in various medical forms, notably leuk(h)aemia, white blood. More happily we find it in generic names, Latinised and so spelt with a -c-. *Leucadendron argenteum*, known to us as the silver tree, inspired the generic name.

Cyananthus "Trailing bellflower" *Campanulaceae* c.30 species. This is the blue flower. Most species are one shade or another of blue. We may be less familiar with *cyan-* blue, but there it is in cyanide, which has elements that are bluish. "Blue babies" born with insufficient oxygen in the blood, have cyanosis.

Chrysanthemum   *Compositae* 5 species. Once a genus of about a hundred species, this has lately been refined, reduced by botanists, many species being placed now in other genera. The colour range is now wide, though when Linnaeus chose this name, gold, *chrys-*, was predominant. We find *chrys-* in chrysalis – a touch of poetry here: inside that dull brown bag, hanging in the garden is a creature, moth or butterfly, preparing to emerge, gold dusted!

Helichrysum   "Everlasting flower"   "Straw flower"   "Curry plant" *Compositae* 500 species. This is *helios*, sun *chrys-* gold; or, as some dictionaries suggest, it is, not *helios*, sun, but *helix*, spiral. Have you ever seen the petals spiral sideways? Anyway, helix used by us usually appears as *helico-* most familiar in helico/pter, spiral wings. Curry plant refers to H. *angustifolium* which gives off a strong smell of curry. (C16)

Viola "Violet" "Pansy" "Heartsease" *Violaceae* 500 species.   The Romans knew this flower and called it *viola*, a word related to the earlier Greek *ion*. We include the genus here because for the Romans *viola* also meant colour. From the French we have violet (little *viola*) and pansy. This last, originally in English spelt *ponsay* is from *pensée*, French, thought. That pensive little face, with its quizzical eyebrows, inspired the name ... and now we all know that "pansies are for thoughts". Heartsease refers to the healing properties of this plant which has been used medicinally from the days of Hippocrates. Broadly speaking violets have strap-shaped petals, and pansies broader, rounded ones.

Chlorophytum "Spider Plant" *Liliaceae* 215 species. Chlorophytum means green plant. Most species have evergreen foliage. We are familiar with *chloros*, Greek, green from the chlorine in our swimming baths, and from chlorophyll, the colouring matter in the green part of plants. Why *-phytum*? The Greek word for plant is *botane* – hence our botany and botanical gardens. They also had *phyton*, which we use as *-phyte*,
a living organism, a lesser plant.
And the feature of this genus is the
little plantlets, which, like spiders,
hang in mid-air at the end of stems.

Nigella "Love-in-a-mist" *Ranunculaceae* 14 species.   Though
nigella is but a small genus of annual herbs, it is a popular garden
plant, a love-blue flower veiled in its own green mist. It was there
every
summer in my
childhood home
bringing for me
thoughts of
gentle romance –
lovers wandering
lost in
their dreams,
their kisses
as soft as
the mist itself.
      I now know
that that mist
is made up
of the feathery bracts
that surround the flower
of N. *damascus* of southern Europe.
      The genus ranges widely
throughout Eurasia.
      So why nigella? We associate Nigeria
with black people, and so it is named,
from *niger*, Latin, black. To denigrate is
to blacken, usually a reputation . . .
and our plant? The seed pod is very
striking. When ripened it is inflated
and pale brown; but within can be found
seeds that are black indeed and very small –
hence that ending -ella. Nigella is a good
name for the keen botanist or the observant gardener.

      This flower had her beauty ignored. Now to some plants that are
indeed named for their beauty.

Beauty

Our word beauty comes to us from French, which gives us *beau* and *belle*, but the final source is Latin *bellus*, related to *bonus*, good. The Greek word for beauty is *kallos*; for beautiful, *kalos*. From this we have calligraphy, beautiful writing, callisthenics, (exercises for) beautiful strength. When we keep the original Greek *k-* we have kaleidoscope, beautiful form to look at. Plant names follow.

Bellis "Daisy" *Compositae* c.17 species. Daisy is from Old English. It means the day's eye. It opens in the morning and closes at night – a touch of poetry here – but *bellis* it is, pretty one. The lawn weed B. *perennis* has given rise to many garden species.

Calanthe *Orchidaceae* c.120 species. This is easily translated: beautiful flower. A genus of orchids, these flowers range through pink-purple to white, and they are very showy, appearing four-lobed, because the lip has three clefts.

Callistephus "China aster" *Compositae* 1 species. Though a genus of but one species, there are many varieties, and a characteristic is the attractive, sometimes quilted, central disc. They are named beautiful crown. For *stephanos*, crown, see the chapter Shapes, page 21.

Calluna "Heather" *Ericaceae* 1 species. Here we come down to the very practical, for while *kalos* means beautiful, *kalluna* means I adorn. This name refers not only to the beauty of the flower but also to the fact that the stems were used to make brooms to sweep the house and make it beautiful!

Callitris "Bribie Island Pine" *Cupressaceae* 17 species. Examine the leaves here – they come in threes – hence that ending *-tris*. Beautiful to look at, these trees also produce wonderful wood, believed by the Turks to be indestructible and so used by them for the floors and ceilings of their mosques.

Callistemon and **callicarpa** are to be found under Stamen and Fruit respectively, pages 12 and 13. A special note about calla, often called arum lily: calla, beautiful one, is now zantedeschia written of in *Gentlemen in my Garden*.

Age

Throughout our lives age is important to us. Shining eyes express the joy of the small child when the 'birfday' comes along; to be 'thix' or 'theven' is toothless triumph. The pride continues. At adolescence the young woman is moulded; the young man more squarely etched … Proud fingers touch the stubbling chin. We finally come of age, but so soon thereafter find old age itself has a foot in the door! However, with old age comes dignity if we consider the language.

From *old*, we English have elders and aldermen. The Romans had the same idea. For them to be old was to be *senex*. They filled the senate with senators. Americans today follow suit. While senile is diminutive and derogatory, mildly implying a downgrading, senior is complimentary. Sir and sire are derivatives. When we turn to the Greek we find the same idea. *Presbus*, old man, denotes seniority, for us the source of priest and Presbyterian – but no plant names. Another word for old age, *geras*, we know in geriatric, old and in need of a physician, *iatros*. With these thoughts in mind perhaps we are better prepared for the plant names that follow.

Senecio *Compositae* c.1000 species.   It's hardly possible to find a garden without senecio. I love it for that touch of grey. *Senecio* is interesting in that it was a Roman family name. Someone in the family must have looked especially old – or dignified. The genus senecio includes annuals, perennials, succulents, shrubby varieties, climbers and weeds and is distributed throughout most of the world. The name refers to the white or grey hair-like seeds appearing after flowering. Even with a thousand species, you still may not grow a senecio in your garden. Hunt out ragwort, S. *jacobea*, a most troublesome noxious weed. Or perhaps, inadvertently you grow S. *vulgaris*, literally the common one – that weed we call groundsel, the favoured host of the black hairy caterpillar. Some gardeners let this grow to feed the seed to cage birds. See the flower-head. It is tubular, a long narrow cylinder which in due time, holds the downy seeds in place. Here you have it – an aureole of light, like the fine, white hair that crowns the heads of some old people.

Sempervivum   "Houseleek"   "Hen and chickens"   *Crassulaceae*
42 species. Great tenacity to life inspired the name *sempervivum*, Latin,
life for ever! Discarded plants thrown onto a heap can be found
months later extending hopeful roots into the air! Moreover, like a
hen with chickens there are always little ones around. And houseleek?
These plants are grown on roofs sometimes to prevent lightning
strike.

Ageratum   *Compositae* 43 species. In effect this has the same
meaning as sempervivum, for it is *a-*, without, *geras*, old age. Individual
flowers last particularly well and blooming is from early spring till the
late frosts arrive.

Amaranthus   "Love-lies-
bleeding"   "Prince's feather"
Amaranthaceae c.60 species.
Every woman wants to have
amaranthine beauty. Some
achieve this. Qualities
of character
become etched in
facial lines; white
hair haloes beauty
that has not faded but
rather grown with the
years. Amaranthine comes
from *a-*, not, *marantos*,
fading ... everlasting. While
the plumes on love-lies-
bleeding,
A. *caudatus* (pictured), are long and
drooping conjuring thoughts of
someone wounded for love
and dying, the plumes of prince's
feather, A. *hypochondriacus*, ride
high as a prince's feather should.
Some flowers appear to be everlasting.
This is a name to be appreciated.

Shapes

Greeks and Romans walk in our houses and gardens, trailing their history and habits – and we fail to recognise them. There follows a collection of plant genera where the name inevitably leads us to those earlier peoples.

Aspidistra "Parlour palm" *Liliaceae* 8 species. Think of a Greek in fearful self-defence behind his shield, *aspis*. While most sources say that it is those marvellous leaves which inspire the name, some say that it is the mushroom-shaped stigma which characterises the genus. (C19)

Gladiolus "Sword lily" *Liliaceae* c.180 species. Think of the Romans, crowding the Colosseum, shouting at the sight of the gladiators, fighting to the death with the sword, *gladius*. Gladiolus is little sword, not the real thing; but how sword-like are those leaves, and even the sheaf of buds. A good name. (C16)

Cistus "Rock rose" *Cistaceae* c.20 species. Ritual objects were important in ancient Greece and Rome, and after use were put away in *kiste*, a box. In archeology a kist or cist is a burial chamber. This plant has seed capsules like boxes. *Kistos* is Greek for rock rose.

Calceolaria "Slipper flower" *Scrophulariaceae* c.300 species. In a Roman street you could know who were senators by their footwear! While the people of the countries the Romans occupied often went barefoot, the Romans never did. Regular soldiers wore sandals, but senators wore a special type of shoe, *calceus*. It was a proud day when a newly appointed senator was allowed to change shoes. *Calceus mutare* meant to become a senator. Today certain monks and nuns are discalced. They wear no proper shoes, sandals at most, and often go barefoot. While *calceus* is shoe, *calceolus* is little shoe, that is a slipper, and the flowers of many species of this genus are like big, soft, fat, comfortable slippers. (C18)

Fritillaria   *Liliaceae*   c.100 species. Even the serious Romans had their fun and played at games of dice. Rattling these in a dice-box, *fritillus*, they saw this as being *frivolus*, frivolous, and these two words are related. Consider all this as you look at fritillaria. Flowers are empty and bell-like, with markings like those we are familiar with on dice. (C17)

Passiflora   "Passion flower"   *Passifloraceae* c.500 species. The Romans put their enemies to death by crucifixion. This they did to the Christ, while soldiers played dice. Christ being crowned with thorns and crucified is remembered by all Christian peoples; and when America was discovered and this native flower was seen by Spaniards for the first time, it reminded them of the Passion or suffering of Christ – the bloom's spiny centre looked like the crown of thorns; symbols of the nails and the cross seemed plain, and even the ten petals were seen to represent ten of the twelve apostles, the two left out being Peter who denied Him and Judas who betrayed Him. Perhaps we do not think of this when we purchase passion fruit from the market.

Monstera   "Swiss cheese plant"   "Fruit salad plant"   *Araceae* 22 species. The Romans believed in omens, portents, apparitions. Their word was *monstrum*, from which we take our word monster. Monstera is named from the odd appearance of its curiously perforated leaves. Swiss cheese plant is not a bad name either! Fruit salad plant, M. *deliciosa*, has fruit that is edible.

Dracaena   "Dragon tree"   *Agavaceae* c.40 species. The Greeks had the dragon, *drakon*, and the female dragon, *drakaina*! and it's this last which is the inspiration here. In the Canary Islands is *Dracaena drago*, a great tree which oozes red resin, has trunk and branches of grotesque form and has lived, it is thought, for a thousand years! A she-dragon indeed! There are milder species.

Stephanotis   "Clustered wax flower"   *Asclepiadaceae* c.5 species. A triumphant Greek was apt to wear a crown, *stephanos*. These tender, evergreen, twining shrubs, with waxy, white fragrant flowers are much used by florists for bouquets. The ending *-otis* means eared; there are ear-like processes on the crown of the stamens. See Callistephus page 17.

Tropaeolum "Nasturtium" "Indian cress" *Tropaeolaceae* 88
species.
Have you ever wiggled your nose at a bit of cress, sharp and pungent?
Pliny did, and so he named a certain cress nasturtium,
nas- nose, *turt-*, twister. All that was long ago. When the New World
opened up, a wonderful new plant was discovered in South America –
Peru to be exact. Its smooth leaves, its flowers and stalks, sharply
pungent, could be used much as cress is used. It was given the name
nasturtium. At a later stage gardeners often grew one species, T. *major*,
up netted poles – which gave Linnaeus an idea. Why not call this
genus Tropaeolum?

Here's the story: in ancient Greece after a one-day battle, the
conqueror would hang the shield and helmet of the vanquished
leader on a trophy pole, called the *tropaeolum*. These gleamed in the
setting sun. For Linnaeus the leaves were shields, and those
marvellous flowers were bright helmets. Our word trophy comes
from that old word *tropaeolum*. We still hold trophies aloft.

There's much to think about as we sit in the garden and munch
on a bit of T. *majus* – "Indian cress". We could use it more ourselves
– the young leaves as vegetables, and the pungent petals in
salads.

Illustration by Andrew Francis

22

Canna *Cannaceae* 9 species.   Cannas stand, bright and tall, in summer gardens here, often arranged in serried rows according to their height and colour – red, orange, yellow. The story of their name is just as colourful. Of the nine species most have been superceded by hybrid plants, but all the original plants are from tropical America. Their very Old World name is inspired by those stalks, from *canna*, Latin, reed or cane – pipe or flute. We've much to pipe about in the story of this word, for the Romans took it from the Greeks, who took it from the Assyrians – or possibly the Hebrews – who took it from the early Sumerians. English words from this source abound: cane, canister (made from cane), cannabis, cannelloni (Italian tubular pasta), cannula in surgery (a small pipe for outlet of fluids), war cannons, canal – very Italian – and its French counterpart, channel. Here come the Spaniards with canyon, so common in hilly Spain. … Our list is incomplete. When your cannas have died down for the winter you've much to think about before those tall canes appear again.

Campanula "Bellflower" "Canterbury bell" *Campanulaceae* 300 species.   In this country we have campanologers or bell-ringers, skilled in the art of campanology, but there are many more in Europe. Campanologers go deaf with their trade … we all recall the hunchback of Notre Dame. In Italy particularly, where bell-ringing is so important, the bell-tower or campanile often stands apart from the church. While in Latin *campana* is bell, *campanula* is little bell, an apt name for this genus, though there are two distinct flower types – star-shape and bell-shape. While many star-shaped varieties are hardly like little bells, others truly are. Here is a story. During the Middle Ages pilgrims were attracted to Canterbury, to the shrine of Thomas à Beckett, that bishop so beloved of his people, but murdered in his own cathedral in 1170. The journeying pilgrims attached small bells to their horses – bells not unlike the flowers we know so well. It is C. *medium* that is called the Canterbury bell.

Linum "Flax" *Linaceae* c.200 species. Linum does not of itself belong among shapes. It has become a shape. What the English called flax the Romans called *linum*, and because of its many uses *linum* also meant a thread, rope, fishing line. ... It is natural that from this source English words flow: line itself, shipping and air lines; lineage, which is ancestral line; lineaments, the outline, usually of the face; and we outline, delineate; align and realign (through French). Lining was once always of linen. Linseed is the favourite food of the linnet! To our plant: L. *usitatissimum*, literally the common flax, the one most often *used*, has been valued for millennia by Romans, Greeks, Hebrews, Egyptians and others for many purposes. It is this species which has given rise to so much language. You may not grow this in your garden, but within this genus, native throughout the northern regions, there are many garden varieties. Personally I like that Old English word flax. As you say it you can almost hear it flapping in the wind!

Cyclamen "Persian violet" "Alpine violet" "Sowbread" *Primulaceae* 19 species. Cyclamen grows naturally in every country and island with a Mediterranean coastline – freely in the open, under trees, in the shade of rocks. Of nineteen species some are scented. I like to think of some Minoan princess of long ago, walking in the early morning air, beneath the Aegean sky, making her selection – pink, white or purple flowers? plain or marbled leaves? It's suitable that this flower should have a Grecian name, but why a name from *cycl–* the Latin form of an older Greek word for circle? The flower is shuttlecock-shaped with petals sharply reflexed! Lexicographers, chin in hand, ponder. The answer lies in the soil! When you knock out your potted plant annually to clear the corm there's your circle! Lexicogaphers give this as the possible reason for the name ... and sowbread? Swine love especially C. *europaeum* and eat the corms.

Capsicum "Peppers" "Cayenne" "Chilli" *Solanaceae* 10 species. We eat capsicums, those glossy, bright fruits, round, ovoid or conical – marvellous in summer salads. We flavour with some. Cayenne pepper, for sprinkling or using sparingly, is made from the dried seed pods of various capsicums, *cayenne* being an Anglicised form of a Tupi (North American Indian) word. *Chilli* is an Aztec word. Some capsicums are highly decorative, so we include the genus here. Chop open your capsicum. It's empty, like an open case, and so named, from *capsa*, Latin, case. Indeed, case itself has the same source, through the French, *caisse*. The closest word for us in English is capsule, little case, familiar to us in medicine. In botany the capsule is the dry fruit that liberates the seed: or capsules may be the spore-producing parts of mosses or liverworts. A capsule can also be a space-craft! From small beginnings this language flies high; and we've tried to encapsulate a few ideas so for you so capsicum is better understood.

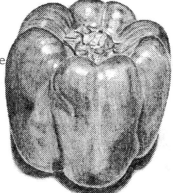

Note: Some sources say that capsicum comes from *kapto*, I bite, referring to the pungency of some peppers. Who bites whom, I wonder.

Tulipa "Tulip" *Liliaceae* c.300 species. We leave the Greeks and Romans now and come to a Turkish shape. You could be forgiven for thinking that the tulip was native to Holland. Many people do, but its homeland is Turkey. The Turks loved this flower, and in earlier times it was customary at evening parties to fit little lamps on the backs of tortoises and let them creep among the flower beds. There's a story to tell of the tulip. In 1554 an ambassador visiting Istanbul (then Constantinople) was conferring among turbanned heads when in a moment of leisure he saw a flower he'd never seen before. He was enchanted. It's a long story, but twenty years later the plant was brought to Europe. Introduced to Holland it thrived there and changed the history of that country. Tulip, the word is colourful. Its origin is the Turkish word for turban – and every flower rounds out from the base, closing in again at the top, just like a turban.

Creatures

With such a wide variety in shape and form among the various creatures in the world, it's no wonder we use them in garden language, the creature itself, or sometimes one of its parts. Hiding in generic names these are there to surprise us, to delight, to charm, to inform. Let's get introduced.

Geranium "Cranesbill" *Geraniaceae* 300 species. For the Greeks the crane was *geranos*, and so they named *geranion*, geranium. During flowering, look for those fruits shaped like a crane's bill. Good for the Greeks!

Pelargonium "Storksbill" *Geraniaceae* 250 species. What more natural when this similar but separate genus was discovered in South Africa, than to coin pelargonium, from Greek *pelargos*, stork.

Ranunculus "Buttercup" "Common water crowfoot" *Ranunculaceae* 400 species. In Latin *rana* is frog, *ranunculus*, little frog. We are familiar with *-unculus*, a diminutive, Anglicised to -uncle, in carbuncle, a little coal or carb, burning in your skin; and in peduncle, little foot, a botanical term. To our plant: "little frog" – many species inhabit marshy places as do frogs. Pliny (c.23–79 AD), coined this name.

Hippeastrum "Amaryllis" "Knight's star lily" *Amaryllidaceae* 80 species, all bulbous. What a name! What imagery! but it needs a little sorting out. The hippopotamus is the *hippo-*, horse, of the *potamus*, river. Horseman is *hippeas*. Hippeastrum is a coalescence of *hippeas* and *aster*, star. The large, star-shaped, six-petalled flowers ride high on strong stalks.

Echinops "Globe thistle" *Compositae* c.120 species. Globe thistle aptly describes this genus, with thistle-like leaves and flowers that are spiny globes of metallic lustre. These round prickly globes make you think of a hedgehog, in Greek *echinos* – easy to remember because from *echin-* we name our urchins, with their stand-up hair! Echinops means looking like a hedgehog, all rolled up and very tidy.

Arctotis "African daisy" *Compositae* c.50 species. From *arktos*, Greek, bear, we the name the arctic, because of the constellation the Great Bear. So *arct-* of arctotis means bear. Observe the woolly leaves and stems. But what of -*otis*? If you've ever had the mumps, that great swelling was in your parotid glands, *para*, beside, -*ot*, the ear. The otologist is the ear specialist. Arctotis, then, is bear's ear. Have a look at the form of the fruit.

Lupinus "Lupin" "Lupine" *Leguminosae* 200 species.   For the Romans the wolf was *lupus*, and for them *lupinus* was the wolf-bean, the plant we know as lupin, and so the word is old. The genus lupinus is wild. It was once thought that it exhausted the soil rapidly and hence it was compared to a greedy wolf. It was misjudged. The fact is it can thrive on already poor soils. Moreover, like other legumes, it possesses nitrogen-fixing nodules on its roots and is very beneficial to the soil. We would not, however, have lupin in our gardens were it not for George Russell (1867–1935) who, by vigorous selection of seed-raised plants produced the Russell strain. (C14)

Onosma "Golden drop" *Boraginaceae* c.150 species.   Rough, hairy foliage on these perennial sub-shrubs does not put off the ass, *onos*, for he loves the smell of the tubular almond-scented flowers! And so they are named, *onos*, ass, *osmē*, smell. The onager or wild ass is literally the ass, *onos*, of the field, *agros*. This connection helps us to remember *onos*, ass. We recall it too in *Onopordum*, the generic name for the Scotch thistle. Onopordum means asses consume!

Ornithogalum "Chincherinchee" "Star of Bethlehem" *Liliaceae* c.80 species.   This bulbous genus has three most special names. Chincherinchee refers to O. *thyrsoides* of South Africa. The long fleshy leaves whistle in the wind, rubbing together, murmuring "Chincherinchee, chincherinchee". Star of Bethlehem conjures visual imagery, for most flowers are white, at least twenty centimetres across and vividly star-shaped. The generic name, used by the ancient Greeks, has equal beauty. It's those flowers! A stem can carry twenty to thirty, white, cream or yellow – conjuring in the mind a flock of milk-white birds, from *ornith-*, bird and *gal-*, milk.

Leontopodium "Edelweiss" *Compositae* 5 species.   In Greek lion is *leo, leonto-*. For -*pod-* foot, see the chapter Body Parts, page 38. Lion's paw is very picturesque. L. *alpinum* has flower stems covered with dense white woolly hairs, and the flowers themselves are closely surrounded with petal-like woolly bracts. *Edelweiss*, from German, means noble and white – a good popular name for this flower of the mountains, so loved, so praised in song.

Myosotis "Forget-me-not" *Boraginaceae* 50 species. Myosotis! a cryptic word indeed for a flower as simple as the forget-me-not, spreading its blanket of baby-blue beneath the trees or out in the sunlight, in spring or in early summer. We might prefer the name forget-me-not with its accompanying legend. An ardent lover was taking a bouquet to his sweetheart. He had to cross a river, missed his footing, fell, and was carried away in the current to his death. As his bouquet floated gently on the waters, his voice was heard to call, "Forget-me-not!"

Myosotis is no longer puzzling when we split it up, *myos-*, mouse; *-otis*, ear. The mouse has been with us for millennia, named in Sanskrit from a word meaning to steal! It has inspired language. The Latin form is *mus*, from which we name our muscles, little mice, from the fancied mouselike shape of some muscles. In this generic name we turn to the Greek form, *myos*. For *-otis*, ear, see Arctotis, page 26. Mouse ear? Run your fingers over the soft, furry leaves, the reason for the name. Homelands are largely European though some species are from New Zealand.

Myosotidium "Chatham Islands Forget-me-not" *Boraginaceae* 1 species. Myosotidium ends with *-idium* from *idem*, the same. Relate this word to identical, which also comes from *idem*. The flowers of the ordinary forget-me-not and this special one are similar.

Coreopsis "Tickseed" *Compositae* 80 species. Free flowering, upright and busy, with colourful daisy-like flowers, these plants thrive in smoky industrial areas. There are both hardy annuals and perennials and homelands are North and South America. Tickseed makes you scratch your head! So should coreopsis. Here's the story: *aphis*, bane of the gardener's life, was first introduced to us by Linnaeus – the word that is, but it should be *koris*. Long before the time of Linnaeus, some copyist wrote *aphis* instead of *koris* – in the Greek script the two words look alike. So Linnaeus, copying, gave us aphis. Now to our plant: *koris* + *opsis*, coreopsis, means looking like a bug. Beauty and great qualities have been ignored. Someone has seen that the seeds look like bugs – not your innocent bug, but a bedbug! (C19)

Delphinium "Larkspur" "Rocket larkspur" *Ranunculaceae* c.250 species. Into the air an arrow of blue! So shoots the dolphin! So too does delphinium; and each floret has a nectary deep-set, like the eye of a dolphin. The ancient Greeks named these flowers *delphinion*, from *delphis*, dolphin. The dolphin has always been loved. It provided the French centuries ago with inspiration for the family name *Dauphin* which, from 1349–1830, became the title of the direct heir to the throne. We've a top class name here. What of the plant? This genus consists of annual, biennial and perennial herbs, and homelands range from the Mediterranean to Siberia. Larkspur occurs because some species have most noticeable spurred petals. All larks, especially the skylark, have spurs. The original colours have been added to with red and even yellow. For my part that shoot of blue is enough! (C17)

Echium "Pride of Madeira" "Paterson's curse" "Viper's bugloss" *Boraginaceae* 40 species. Spectacular to look at, spectacular in names. Most species have very tall, flowered stems, and in the wild some can grow to five metres. Pride of Madeira says all. This plant, E. *candicans*, a robust shrub with tapering, densely flowered spikes, makes a splendid feature plant. It's a different story with Paterson's curse, E. *plantagineum*. For all its Mediterranean beauty, this quickly became a noxious weed in the warmer parts of south Australia. Viper's bugloss, E. *vulgare*, literally the common one, has a different bushy habit, its great profusion of violet blue flowers giving a misty beauty to sand-hills and other wild places where it thrives. Bugloss, a shortened form of Greek *bouglossus*, ox-tongued, is applied to various plants in the borage family. And so to viper, in Greek *echion*. We say echium. This genus is named after the viper either because of a supposed cure for snake bite, or because the seeds are the shape of a viper's head. Both reasons are given. I prefer the latter. I've proved it. Homelands include Europe, the Canary Islands, Africa and west Asia.

Aquilegia "Granny's bonnet" "Columbine" *Ranunculaceae* 70 species.

Granny's bonnet! a pastel shaded flower with five spurred petals. ... We can just see granny hurrying along in her best bonnet, ribbons flying! Columbine also touches the heart; the inverted flower resembles a group of five doves; from *columba*, Latin, dove. We've cameos of beauty and clarity here. Not so when it comes to aquilegia ... only confusion. Most dictionaries give the name columbine, but note that the meaning of aquilegia is unknown. Let's have a nosey around. In England up until the seventeenth century anyone could have a beaked nose, but from that time on it was more likely to be aquiline! from Latin, *aquila*, eagle. Poets seized upon the word, and about that time aquilegia entered the English language. Appreciate those spurred petals on this flower from north temperate regions. (C16)

Ipomoea "Morning glory" *Convolvulaceae* c.500 species. Morning glory! A beautiful name for this climbing plant, out of tropical America, especially Mexico. The flowers, usually trumpet-shaped, tend to be violet or purple, bright in the morning, but fading in the afternoon. The genus includes annuals, perennials and shrubs, as well as the climbers. The *kumara* or Maori potato, I. *batatas*, is a climber with a tuberous rootstock, and an important food source in tropical areas. We look for a connecting link. We ask why ipomoea? This is coalescence of two words from Greek, *ipo-*, worm and *-homo*, the same as, or like. It's like that little curling tendril, so like the ordinary garden worm. (For the Greeks the intestinal worm was helminth; we'll leave helminthology to the medical profession.) As you watch the progress of your ipomoea note those thin twining stems carrying your flowers to great heights. Hail to the twirly worm. (C18) (Linnaeus)

The Beneficent World

The world is wide, its beauties and products lavish. What of the moon and the stars, the sea and the cosmos itself. What of fire, flame and ash, water and dew, chalk and sand? Plant names follow.

Lunaria "Honesty" *Cruciferae*
3 species. The moon slips
silently across the night sky
and lovers go crazy. Indeed
it was once
thought that
lunacy,
particularly the
intermittent kind
was caused by the
phases of the moon,
in Latin, *luna*.
We've luna moth,
lunar rainbow, lunate bone
in the wrist ... but why this
plant which most people call honesty? It's those
marvellous seed-heads – great, round, wide, honest
moon-faces, yielded by two species. Pick a mature
seed-head. Rub each circle between finger and thumb and release the
outer covering to reveal a silvery moon!

Arenaria "Sandwort" *Caryophyllaceae* c.160 species. This brings
us down to earth. Arena, the word suggests to us perhaps the political
arena, where blood is seldom spilt; but in the original arena blood *was*
spilt – in the centre of the great Colosseum, where gladiators fought
to the death and Christians were thrown to the lions. It was called the
arena because it was sprinkled with sand, *arena*, (strictly *harena*) to
soak up the blood. Arenaria simply likes dry places, thriving in rock
gardens or alpine houses. It is low-growing, creeping and mat-
forming.

Cineraria *Compositae* c.50 species. Sometimes classed among the senecios, this is noted as a genus in the Royal Horticultural Society Dictionary. From *ciner-* Latin, ash, we name our incinerators, turning all to ash. Here it is the ashen appearance on the back of the leaves which gives rise to the name.

Pyracantha "Firethorn" *Rosaceae* 7 species.   The ultimate *pyr–* is the funeral pyre, from the Greek word for fire, but there are pyrotechnics to delight the eye and many *pyr-* words. Here *pyr-* refers to the fiery berries, much favoured by birds. For *-acantha* see Thorn on page 13. Firethorn is a perfect translation. (Perhaps we should note pyrethrum here – no longer a genus in its own right, but its *pyr-* relates to the fires of the body – fevers, its popular name being feverfew. Pyrethrum, the word, will live on in the useful insecticide it produces.) (C17)

Phlox *Polemoniaceae* 67 species.   *Phlox* is the Greek word for flame. Watch the fire in campfire or home grate and see the colours there – blue, magenta, purple, pink or white – and so phlox blooms; and the petals are salver shaped and sometimes cleft like flame, the flowers freely borne. While there are many unpleasant words in medicine beginning *phl-* suggesting inflammation, we can recall the fabled River of Fire in Hades, the Phlegathon; and note that this is a New World flower – North American – with a marvellous Old World name.

Rosmarinus "Rosemary" *Labiatae* 2 species.   For the Romans the sea was *mare*, giving us marines, marinas and marinated foods! For them the dew was *ros*. Rosmarinus, dew of the sea, is a name full of poetic imagery – blue droplets shimmering on waves of green – a wonderful name for a plant growing all round the Mediterranean in the salt sea spray. The Romans named and introduced *rosmarinus* to Britain long ago. The tall upright plant R. *officinalis* is the one so useful herbally. Rosemary is a reverential adaptation to signify the rose of the Virgin Mary.

Gypsophila *Caryophyllaceae* c.100 species.   Gypsophila is a lovely springy word which seems to suit the plant, with its tiny flowers dancing on the stalk, like chickweed, but it has a serious gardening message. Gypsum is a white mineral of common occurrence, with a number of commercial uses: one fine-grained, white or translucent variety is alabaster; another, used for plaster of Paris, was for a long time quarried in the Montmartre district of that city. For us, more importantly, gypsum is added to some fertilisers. Gypsophila, by definition, is gypsum-loving.

Aster *"Michaelmas daisy" Compositae* 250 species.   Astrology is the study of the stars' supposed effect upon humanity. Certainly a dis*aster* is something that goes against our stars! Astronomy is the study of *nomos*, the law, the arrangement of the heavenly bodies. Astronauts are nautical folk among the stars. We've made Greek *aster* very much our own. So what of aster the plant? The flowers are silvery, pinky, purply, and on a clear night the stars twinkle so, a touch of poetry in this name. Michaelmas daisy, A. *novi-belgii*, reflects history for its flowering occurs in England at the time of the feast of St Michael, 29th September. This is but one species in a genus of hardy herbaceous perennials, where flower size varies greatly, as do both colour and height. Homelands include South America, Eurasia, Africa and Asia.

Cosmos *Compositae* c.26 species.   The Greeks would not have known the cosmos. Its homelands are tropical and warm America, especially Mexico. For the Greeks *cosmos* was the world as an ordered whole – that which has emerged from *chaos*. There's thought here: if, from our word world you remove the w- and the -r- you have old, the Anglo-Saxon view of it. The Greek mind goes a little further. *Cosmos* for them meant also order and beauty. There's a true reverence within the word. (In today's society of course, the cosmetic industry does its best to bring order and beauty out of otherwise chaos!) We noted above that we have astronauts. Russians have cosmonauts. We are not alone in borrowing from the Greeks. So what of this genus of annuals and perennials, showy and free-flowering? The ordered centre perhaps and the wavy, uncertain edges of most flowers. Certainly the colours range through crimson, deep rose, pink and gold – colours of the sunset, colours we see in the heavens. (C17)

Hydrangea *Hydrangeaceae* 100 species. Words beginning with hydr-, water, abound in our language, a couple of pages of them in most dictionaries. The second half of hydrangea, *-ang*, signifies vessel, from Greek *angeion*. In medicine an angiogram is a *-gram* or recording of the condition of a blood or lymph vessel. In botany we have angiosperms, plants with seeds in a vessel. See the chapter Seed, page 8.

So why is a hydrangea a water vessel? Some will tell you that hydrangeas wilt badly in the garden when deprived of water. Others assure you that if the picked flowers are placed head down in water for a few hours before arrangement they will last much longer. Both may be true, but the botanical reason given is that the seed-heads have a cup-like formation. With homelands in North and South America and in the East, this is a genus of deciduous and evergreen flowering shrubs; and there are some climbers of branching habit, which cling by means of aerial roots. Linnaeus named this in 1753.

Body Parts

Plant names often sound like medical terms, and why not ... medicine uses Greek and Latin for body parts, and botany uses those parts to describe the appearance or some characteristic of a plant. Amusement can be found, not only in the range of body parts used, but also in the part of the plant that inspires the name – root, leaf, stalk, pappus hairs, spores, petals, seed-heads or individual flowers.

In this chapter we come across a botanical name change common enough, when a genus – one we know and love – disappears entirely in a re-sorting, a re-classification of plants. One such is cheiranthus, wallflower, handflower. No longer a genus in its own right, it's been split up into various other genera and therefore has no proper place in this text, but cheiranthus the word and the accompanying legend are worth recording. Cheiranthus translates literally as the handflower, earlier folk so often carrying a posy of it in the hand. The Greek *kheir (cheir)* without the *-e-* is familiar to us in chiropractor, one whose healing work is with the hand. That's all simple, as is wallflower; these plants like walls, self-seeding readily hard against them. Simple also is the old legend. In fourteenth century Scotland, Elizabeth, daughter of the Earl of March, in love with the son of an enemy clan, dropped a wallflower from her castle window – a sign she was ready to elope with him, but later, in her descent she fell to her death. Her grief-stricken lover placed a wallflower in his cap and left Scotland for ever. He disappeared as completely as this genus will in due time, though it does still appear in many plant books.

Now to further plants named after body parts. Earlier we've seen that in Stephanotis, page 21, Arctotis, page 26 and Myosotis, page 28 the *-otis* refers to ear. What of the eye? Eye in Greek is *opthalmos*, from which we have *-ops* and *-opsis*, seen, used to mean looking like. Two plant names follow, ending *-opsis* and *-ops*.

Meconopsis "Himalayan blue poppy" "Welsh poppy" *Papaveraceae* 43 species.   This looks like a poppy, *mecon*, but is a separate genus. It is an example of comparing one plant with another.

Lithops "Pebble plant" "Living stone" *Aizoaceae* 35 species. These look exactly like the stones among which they grow. Here the plant is compared to an extraneous thing, *lithos*, stone.

Now what of the tooth? While dentist is from Latin, *dent-* tooth, orthodontist is from Greek *ortho-* straight, *odonto-* tooth. We find *odonto-* useful in plant names.

Odontoglossum *Orchidaceae* c.100 species.   See the petals and the sepals. They have jagged edges like teeth, broad and rounded or pointed and narrow, molars and incisors! The second half of that word, *-glossum* is from the Greek for tongue.

Salpiglossis *Solanaceae* 2 species. The Greek for tongue, *glossa* is also useful in plant names – and in other words as well, a glossary being that list of words we have to get our tongue round! Salpiglossis is a trumpet-shaped flower, with petals that are velvety and often veined in deeper or contrasting colours – crimson, scarlet, orange. A *salpigx* was an ancient Greek trumpet, salpingectomy the surgical removal of the Fallopian tubes, which are somewhat trumpet-shaped. Here the style at the corolla throat resembles a tongue.

Cerastium "Snow in summer" *Caryophyllaceae* 60–100 species. Keratin is that fibrous protein occurring in hair, feathers, claws, hooves and horn, from Greek *keras*, horn. Spelt *ceros*, we find this in rhinoceros, nose of horn. Cerastium, a mat-forming perennial, has seed heads which produce little horns, much more miniscule than those on the rhinoceros!

Antirrhinum "Snapdragon" *Scrophulariaceae* c.40 species.   Anti- here means not so much against, but unlike the usual form; and *rhin-* is nose, as we've seen from rhinoceros above. So antirrhinum means rather like a nose, or snout … and children love these flowers which can be opened and shut, snapping like dragons!

Antennaria *Compositae* c.45 species.   The original antenna was, for the Romans, a sail-yard – the yard on which a sail was extended. Aristotle (384–322 BC) used this in the plural, *antennae*, to name the 'horns' or feelers of insects. Great imagination! In antennaria the pappus hairs of male flowers remind one of insect antennae or feelers.

Haemanthus "Blood lily" "Blood flower" *Amaryllidaceae* 21 species. Evergreen, deciduous bulbs these are named because of the brightness of the flowers, not necessarily full blood colour. *Haem-*, blood we find, without the *-h-* in anaemia, insufficient blood ...

Gasteria *Liliaceae* 14 species.   Gastritis is an *-itis* in the *gaster*, stomach, and we all know about that! Gasteria is a small, almost stemless succulent, grown mostly for the attractive markings on the leaves. The reason for the name appears with the flowers – there's a stomach-like swelling at the base of each.

Nephrolepsis "Sword fern" "Ladder fern" *Oleandraceae* c.30 species.
Nephritis is an *-itis* of the kidney, *nephros*. Leprosy is a scaly disease, named from *lepis*, a scale. What has all this to do with a fern so lavish, so beautiful? Look at the spore cases, like little scales, but kidney-shaped.

Hepatica *Ranunculaceae* c.10 species.   Hepatitis is an *-itis* of the liver, *hepatikos*. These woodland flowers, formerly classed under anemone, have reddish-brown leaves, resembling the liver.

Physalis "Chinese lantern" "Cape gooseberry" *Solanaceae* c.80 species.   On this invasive herbaceous perennial we must look to the lantern-like calyx which bears the fruit. It could be said to be like a bag or bladder and so is named, from Greek *physallis*, bladder.

Mammillaria *Cactaceae* c.150 species.   Being of the cactus family, these plants are spiny, but they are small and globular – marvellously named after the mammary glands. The flowers, usually red, appear in an aureole at the top, and some species, for example M. *elegans*, produce a milky sap.

Omphalodes "Navelwort" "Navelseed" *Boraginaceae* 28 species. This is a pretty little plant, not unlike forget-me-not, suitable for woodland planting or in rock gardens. What the English call the navel, the Romans called *umbilicus* – hence our umbilical cord. The Greek word is *omphalos*. Besides being the mammalian navel, this last meant a certain stone at Delphi, the navel of the world. We're in great company here! Study your own navel if you like, but take a good look also at the seed of navelwort.

Orchis *Orchidaceae* c.35 species. This is but one genus in the whole of *Orchidaceae*, but gives its name to that family. Pliny (c.23–79 AD) chose the name. He likened the tuber to a testicle, in Greek *orkhis*.

Arthropodium "Rengarenga lily" "Pale vanilla lily" *Asphodelaceae* 12 species. The Greek word for foot is *pod*, so like our word which was originally *fot*. The podiatrist is the foot-care person. We place our feet upon podiums. … The Greek joint is *arthron*, familiar enough in arthritis, that *-itis* or inflammation of the joints. Both of these, *pod* and *arthron* are used greatly in plant names. They unite in arthropodium. You will see that the flower stalks, that is, the 'feet', are jointed.

Eremurus "Foxtail" "Desert candle" *Liliaceae* 40–50 species. This plant produces majestic spikes of starry flowers, the whole spike not unlike a thick foxtail, but eremurus it is – lonely tail. Split the word up; it's easier to understand. A hermit, living alone, is also called an eremite! one who is lonely, *eremos*. We've already seen in Anthurium, page 5, that *oura* tail is often spelt *-ur-*. Put the two together and you have an amusing description of this herbaceous perennial – lonely or solitary tail.

Pteris "Fern" "Table fern" *Pteridaceae* c.280 species. We all love our ferns and some of us have pteridomania, a passion for ferns! In Greek *pteris, pterid-* is fern. The genus includes deciduous, semi-green and evergreen ferns, many best grown indoors or in cool greenhouses. We include the genus here, among body parts, because in Greek *pteron* is feather or wing. These two words are so alike as these two items are. We are perfectly familiar with *pter-* feather or wing in *ptero*dactyl, the extinct winged reptile and in helico*pter*, which is literally spiral wings.

Digitalis "Foxglove" *Scrophulariaceae* c.90 species

Digitalis stands alone. For one thing it's condemned in many places as a noxious weed though greatly treasured in many gardens. I love it on the wild sheep country where the rugged hills are cropped close and these plants left untouched, their flower stalks standing tall. In Latin *digitus* is finger (or toe) and because we used to count on these, digit has come to mean any number from 0–9. Digitalis is a coined word meaning thimble. Our digits can fit into this fox (folk's) glove. Of about twenty species it is D. *purpurea* which has acquired great importance. It will be forever associated with an eighteenth century physician, William Withering.

His patient was dying of oedema associated with congestive heart failure, but to his surprise was cured by an old woman of Shropshire,

a herbalist. William was fascinated. He discovered that foxglove was the curative element in a large mixture given, and that it was also poisonous ... so he spent the next ten years perfecting the drug digitalin. His contribution to humanity is boundless. This plant, native throughout Europe, north-west Africa and central Asia, is important medicinally.

Now to plants *named* for their medicinal properties.

Medicinal Properties

In earlier days home remedies were often the only remedies, and the kitchen garden with its stock of medicinal plants was an integral part of family life. If a plant was useful why not have that use enshrined in the generic name? You will note how many are coined or sanctioned by Linnaeus. Where possible the useful species is noted.

Aristolochia "Birthwort" "Dutchman's pipe" *Aristolochiaceae* c.300 species. Link birthwort with aristochlia, a joint word made up of *aristos*, best and *lochia*, birth. Some species were once valued as cleansing herbs for those in childbirth. Dutchman's pipe occurs because some species have a slender curving tube, like a pipe. (Linnaeus)

Scabiosa "Scabious" "Pincushion flower" *Dipsacaceae* 60–80 species. This is the scabies plant. One species, S. *atropurpurea*, was once used to treat scabies. Scabies is from Latin, *scabere*, to scratch! Pincushion flower, the happier title, occurs because the central discs have protruding styles. (C14) (Linnaeus)

Scrophularia *Scrophulariaceae* c.200 species. This is the scrofula plant. *Scrofula*, from Latin, is a little sow, and sows are prone to swellings in the neck. Similar swellings in human beings were once called *scrofulae*, little sows, and this was the plant to cure them! Note the more sophisticated spelling in the plant name. Scrofula, probably a form of tuberculosis and once called the king's evil, is now called tuberculosis of the lymph glands.

Solidago "Golden rod" *Compositae* c.100 species. A solid sounding name this, like solid itself, comes from Latin *solidus*, whole. S. *virgaurea* has long been known as the heathen wound herb. The Saracens used it; American Indians used it; and in the Middle Ages it was known as the gangrene herb. Today solidago tea is used for kidney and bladder complaints. S. *canadensis* is prized in gardens for its perennial beauty. (C18) (Linnaeus)

Angelica *Umbelliferae* c.50 species. Legend has it that an angel revealed the medicinal qualities of A. *archangelica*, no less, to cure a plague. This species is still valued in the kitchen. (C18) (Linnaeus)

Saxifraga *Saxifragaceae* c.370 species. These are low-growing plants, happy on rocks, but they do not, in fact break up the rocks among which they grow. Their name, saxifraga, from Latin *saxum*, rock and *frag-* to break, occurs because Pliny (c.23–79 AD) wrote that some species could break up stones in the bladder. (C15)

Salvia "Sage" *Labiatae* c.900 species. *Salvia splendens* is marvellously named, a species popular in gardens for its bonfire brilliance. However, the cue for the name came from the kitchen cousin, S. *officinalis*, often called sage, now in culinary use, but for long seen as a cure-all. In Latin *salvus* means safe, well, in good health. From *salvia* the French took *sauge*, from which in turn English took sage. (C19) Pliny (c.23–79 AD) named salvia.

Saponaria "Soapwort" "Fuller's herb" *Caryophyllaceae* c.20 species. The fresh leaves and roots of S. *officinalis*, full of saponins, produce a soap-like lather. Soap in Latin is *sapo*. This gentle cleanser is still used in museums to restore old fabrics, and by the textile industry for fulling, cleansing and thickening newly woven fabric. (Linnaeus)

Calendula "Pot marigold" *Compositae* c.20 species. The dried flowers of pot marigold, C. *officinalis*, have long been used medicinally. Arabs fed these to their fine horses to strengthen their blood vessels. It is believed, in similar fashion, women may get help with menstrual or monthly problems. This may account for the name calendula, from *calends*, the first day of the Roman month. It is more likely to be because in their native habitat these plants have flowers all year round. (C19) (Linnaeus)

Reseda "Mignonette" *Resedaceae* 55 species. There's no doubt about the meaning of this name: *Reseda morbis*! Assuage diseases! These were the first words of a charm used when applying this as a poultice for the reduction of tumors. (C18) (Pliny)

Plumbago "Leadwort" *Plumbaginaceae* 15 species. Seize upon that leadwort – from Old English, the *wort* or plant to cure lead poisoning. Plumbers now work in plastic but are called plumbers because they originally worked in lead, Latin, *plumbum*. There's less need now for 'leadwort'.

Our special guests follow, sharply contrasting each other for their medicinal value.

Althaea "Marshmallow" "Hollyhock" *Malvaceae* 12 species. Homelands range from west Europe to central Asia. A. *officinalis* interests us here – a wild plant of the marshlands, salt or freshwater, and once the basis of the marshmallow we know as a sweet. From time immemorial and still today the whole plant is used medicinally, its leaves and roots full of soothing mucilage. Althaea, the perfect generic name, is from the Greek verb *althein*, to heal, related to the Latin verb *alere*, to nourish. This suits a plant which is curative and also, in various countries used as aliment, food … fried up with onions, used as a spring tonic. Note: Hollyhock means holy hock. Though once in this genus it is now classified as *Alcea rosea*.

Alyssum "Sweet alyssum" "Madwort" *Cruciferae*. c.168 species. Alyssum is that sweet little white or mauve flower that pops up in all the cracks along the garden path. Correct, though among the many species alyssum may be an annual, a perennial or an evergreen shrub. Its homelands are Europe, Asia and North Africa. There's more to alyssum than that: Pliny (c.23–79 AD) chose the name from Greek *alysson*, which means without madness. There was a belief that one or more species could cure, not your ordinary, gentle madness, but rabies. Let me tell you a story. In the famous book *The Story of San Michele* by Axel Munthe, that itinerant doctor describes many things, one printed indelibly on his mind. Six Russian peasants had been savagely mauled and bitten by a pack of mad wolves. At the expense of the Tzar they were sent to the *Institute Pasteur*, in Paris. Louis Pasteur was in charge. Most reluctantly they were taken in. As the days went by and madness set in, their eyes burned like coals, their jaws snapped at anyone who approached, their dangerous saliva flowed. Paris shuddered at the news – and at the noise of their howls, heard in the streets below. One night two doctors conferred. Next morning all was quiet. The only cure possible in that time and place was given. Please enjoy the charming nonchalance of your alyssum where it flourishes along your path.

Note: In this chapter *officinalis* appears a number of times. In ancient Rome *officina* was a workshop, a manufactory. Any species named *officinalis* has at some time been used to manufacture a useful product.

Characteristics

Characteristics are sometimes reflected in the generic name. Once these are recognised the name is easier to remember. A selection follows.

Primula "Cowslip" "Oxslip" "Primrose" "Polyanthus" *Primulaceae* c.400 species. *Slyppe* in Old English was dung. These plants thrived in lush green fields where cattle grazed. Polyanthus is many-flowered. Primula is from Latin *primus*, first and *-uli*, a diminutive. This is 'firstling of spring' – a charming name. (C18)

Impatiens "Touch-me-not" "Busy lizzie" *Balsaminaceae* 850 species. From Latin, very plainly, this is the impatient one – ripe seed-pods burst open when touched!

Mimosa "Humble plant" "Sensitive plant" *Leguminosae* c.400 species. From Latin *mimus*, mime, this is the mimicking one. M. *pudica*, when touched, mimicks fear or repulsion, recoiling or curling right up not unlike a disturbed hedgehog. It is more sensitive over 24°c but quickly resumes its normal shape. (C18) Some acacias, similar in appearance are sometimes incorrectly referred to as 'mimosa'.

Acacia "Wattle" "Mimosa" *Leguminosae* 700–1200 species. From Greek *akakia*, and thought to be related to *ake*, point, this joins many of our words beginning ac – where sharpness is implied – acid, acrimony, acrobat, acme (which gives us acne! through a wrong spelling somewhere), acropolis … See Thorn, page 13. Some species in this genus have spines, sharp or high points. Wattle occurs because Australian settlers used it for wattle and daub housing.

Aconitum "Monkshood" *Ranunculaceae* c.100 species. This genus, particularly A. *napellus*, has hooded purple flowers, hence monkshood. Aconiton is thought to be from Greek *akon*, dart. The juice was used to poison arrows. (C16)

Photinia "Christmas berry" *Rosaceae* c. 60 species. Here we come into the light – *photos*, from Greek, familiar to us in photograph, that recording through light. *Photeinos* is shining; the young foliage gleams bright red.

Lychnis "Campion" "Ragged robin" "Catchfly" *Caryophyllaceae* c.20 species.   We're with the light again. This word is related to *lukhnos*, lamp. The grey felted leaves of L. *coronaria* were once used to make lamp wicks. (C17)

Telopea "Waratah" *Proteaceae* c.4 species.   Still with the light: these magnificent bright crimson blooms can be seen from afar, from *tele-* far, as in telephone, the far sound; and *op-* suggesting something seen. Waratah is the Australian aboriginal name.

Solanum "Potato" "Aubergine" "Nightshade" *Solanaceae* c.1400 species.   Solanum is the Latin word for nightshade; but some authorities go further, stating that *solanum* is derived from the root *sol*, as found in our word solace. Some species have narcotic effects.

Portulaca "Purslane" "Sun plant" *Portulacaceae* 40 species.   From Latin *port-* carry, as in import, and Latin *lac-* milk as in lactate, this means milk-carrying, referring to the milky juice.

Crassula *Crassulaceae* c.300 species.   *Crassus* was a Roman family name ... somebody in the family must have been thick, fat, gross, or stout! the literal meanings of the word. So too is crassula a genus of succulents.

Hamamelis "Witchhazel" *Hamamelidaceae* c.5 species.   Flowering and fruiting at the same time, this is named *hama*, together, and *melon*, fruit. (C19)

Convallaria "Lily of the valley" *Liliaceae* 1 species.   While *vallis* in Latin is valley, *convallis* is sheltered valley. Convallaria thrives in a sheltered spot. (C19)

Hypericum "St John's wort" *Guttiferae* c.400 species.   From Greek *hyper*, over and *ereikē*, heath, this refers to H. *calycinum* which spreads a dense carpet by means of stolons.

Vinca "Periwinkle" *Apocynaceae* 6 species.   From Latin, *vinculum*, a band, this is named for its tough, long shoots, once much used for making wreaths. Vinculum, band, is used in algebra and medicine.

Crataegus "Hawthorn" *Rosaceae* 100–200 species.   Hawthorn is an apt Old English name – haw being the fruit of a hedge plant. Crataegus is from Greek *kratos*, strength. From *kratos* we take the ending -cracy, where we mean strength or power, as in democracy, the power of the people; aristocracy, plutocracy. ... Here *crat-* refers to the strength of the wood, and possibly also to the general toughness of this plant so tolerant of coastal winds and town pollution.

Sedum "Stonecrop" *Crassulaceae* Over 300 species. From Latin, *sedere*, to sit, these plants seem to be sitting, sedentary, as they grow upon the stones. (C15)

Astilbe *Saxifragaceae* 12 species. This word is a put-down! *a-*, without; *stilbos*, glittering. Why note that? We can't all be stars! Astilbe, with its plume-like heads of tiny flowers makes a good *foil* for other, more spectacular plants – say irises around a pool.. Stilbene is used in chemistry, otherwise we have no further use for this bit of Greek. Just this mild insult.

Phormium "New Zealand flax" *Agavaceae* 2 species. In Latin *fer-* means carry. A conifer carries cones; fertile soil carries much! In Greek *phor-* means carry. Semaphore is carrying signs. Relating *fer* and *phor* helps us to remember the meanings. In Greek, *phormium* is basket. Very sensible. On Cook's second voyage the botanists J. R. and G. Forster named *phormium* because the Maori used it for basket making.

Adiantum "Maidenhair fern" "Spleenwort" *Adiantaceae* c.200 species. The beautiful term maidenhair refers to the strong, black, shiny hair-like stalks of this fern, so suitable for growing indoors. It does not refer to the foliage. The generic name does. A/diantum means not wettable. Pop your plant under the kitchen tap to test the validity of that! We have no further use for *diantos*, wettable, in the English language. Spleenwort comes about because this plant was once used for disorders of the spleen. The genus has homelands widespread, including New Zealand, Australia, North and South America, Japan and Nepal.

Asplenium "Spleenwort" "Bird's-nest fern" *Aspleniaceae* c.70 species Asplenium strictly is a medical term, meaning *a-*, without, *-splenium* (disorders of the) spleen; hence also the popular name spleenwort. Both names refer to the old belief that these ferns were useful medicinally against complaints of the spleen. Because that old belief has been discarded we place this genus here near Adiantum. See above. Many of us are familiar with a bird's-nest fern, A. *nidus*, which in the wild truly resembles a bird's nest, growing as an epiphyte among the trees.

Names We Must
Simply Remember

The plants listed below have names we have adopted from a variety of languages – Sanskrit, Arabic, Persian, Hebrew, Ancient Chinese, Mandarin, Japanese, Nepalese, American Indian – and Greek and Latin. They are listed here because there is little – or very little – to which they can be related in English. We must simply remember them. Because of the wide variety of languages used, homelands are also included here.

Abutilon *Malvaceae* 150 species.   Tropics of America, Asia, Africa and Australia. Arabic, for a genus related to mallow. (C18)

Agave "Century plant" *Agavaceae* 300 species.   North and South America. Greek, *agaue*, illustrious, referring to that stately flower-head. It flowers once in 40–60 years, not once a century. (C18)

Aloe *Liliaceae* c.325 species.   Tropical Africa. Greek *aloē*. (C14)

Amaryllis "Belladonna" *Amaryllidaceae* 1 species.   South Africa. Name of a country girl in various Greek poems. (C18)

Arbutus "Strawberry tree" (from the appearance of the berries) *Ericaceae* 14 species.   Western North America, southern and western Europe. Latin *arbutus*, a word related to *arbor*, tree. (C16)

Aucuba *Cornaceae* 3–4 species East Asia. Japanese. (C29)

Berberis *Berberidaceae* 450 species.   Eurasia, Africa and the Americas. From an Arabic word, *berberys*, named for the fruit.

Camassia "Quamash" *Liliaceae* 5–6 species.   North and South America. From Nootka (North American Indian) *chamas*, sweet. The sweet bulb is native food. (C19)

Cassia *Leguminosae* 535 species.   Tropics. Hebrew, *kesi'ah*. Used in Old English.

Ceonothus *Rhamnaceae* 50–60 species.   North America. Greek, *keonothōs*, a spiny plant.

Cestrum *Solanaceae* 175 species. Tropics of South America. Greek, *kestrum*, name of a similar plant.

Cissus *Vitaceae* c.350 species.   A tropical plant, this has a scrambling habit, and is named therefore from Greek *kissos*, ivy. Cissoid is used as a geometric term. See Hedera, page 47.

Clematis "Traveller's joy" "Old man's beard" *Ranunculaceae*
c.200 species.   North and south temperate regions. Greek, *klematis*,
climbing plant, from *klema*, twig. (C16)

Cleome "Spider plant" *Capparidaceae* 150 species.   Pantropical
regions. New Latin, of obscure origin.

Colchicum "Autumn crocus" "Naked ladies" *Liliaceae* 45 species.
Eastern Europe, west Asia, India and China. Kolchis, where this plant
grew, was a region near the Black Sea, where the witch Medea dabbled
in poisonous plants.

Crinum *Amaryllidaceae* 130 species.   Warm and tropical regions.
Greek, *krinon*, an alternative word for lily. See Lilium page 48.

Crocus *Iridaceae* 80 species. Mid- and south Europe, central Asia.
From Greek *krokos*, saffron, ultimately of Semitic origin. (C17)

Datura "Thorn apple" *Solanaceae* 8 species.   Southern North
America, India. D. *stramonium* has prickly fruits. Sanskrit *dhattura*. (C16)

Erica "Heath" "Heather" *Ericaceae* 735 species.   South Africa,
Middle East, Europe. Greek, *ereikē*, heath, from a verb meaning I break,
referring to the brittle stems. (Also, some say, an infusion of the
leaves was reputed to break stones in the bladder!)

Eryngium "Sea holly" *Umbelliferae* 230 species.   Cosmopolitan.
Greek, *erungion*, the diminutive of *erungos*, thistle – so, little thistle.

Genista "Broom" *Leguminosae* 90 species.   Europe to west Asia.
Latin, *genista*, used by Virgil for the broom-plant. (C17)
Extra note: Plantagenet, the name of the kings of England from Henry
II to Richard II, comes from *planta genista*, sprig of broom, worn by an
ancestor as he rode about the country. He wore it jauntily!

Geum "Avens" *Rosaceae* 50 species.   Europe, Asia, New Zealand,
North and South America, Africa. Latin *gaeum*. (C19)

Ginkgo *Ginkoaceae* 1 species.   China. Cultivation elsewhere has
saved this plant from near extinction. From two words in ancient
Chinese, meaning silver apricot.

Hedera *Araliaceae* 11 species.   Europe, Asia, North Africa. Latin,
hedera, ivy. See Cissus, page 46.

Helleborus "Hellebore" "Christmas rose" *Ranunculaceae* 15
species. Europe through to west China. Its poisonous roots inspire
the name from *helein*, to kill, and *bora*, food.

Hibiscus *Malvaceae* c.220 species.   Warm, tropical and subtropical areas. Greek *hibiskos*, Virgil's name for marshmallow. (C18)

Iberis "Candytuft" *Cruciferae* 30 species.   Southern Europe, west Asia. From Iberia, where the genus was supposed to have been found. Early Greek navigators called the Spanish peninsula Iberia.

Ilex "Holly" *Aquifoliaceae* 400+ species.   Temperate and tropical regions. *Ilex* is Latin for holm-oak, the evergreen oak, which has holly-like young leaves. *Quercus, aesculus,* and *robur* (the robust one), are other Latin names for oaks. Holm and holly are related words.

Ixia *Iridaceae* 45–50 species.   South Africa. In Greek *ixos* is mistletoe and *ixia* the bird-lime made from its berries. Here the reference is to the sticky juice in this plant. (C18)

Jacaranda *Bignoniaceae* c.40 species.   Tropical America. From the Brazilian name. (C18)

Jasminum "Jasmine" *Oleaceae* c.200 species.   Temperate and tropical Old World. From Persian, *yāsmīn.* (C16)

Kalanchoe *Crassulaceae* 125 species.   Tropics, especially the Old World. Mandarin, tall, cool, plant.

Laburnum "Golden chain" *Leguminosae* 2 species.   South Europe, west Asia. Pliny (23–79 AD) named this plant. (C16)

Lantana *Verbenaceae* 150 species.   Tropical Americas and Africa. From its superficial similarity to *Viburnum lantana.* (C18)

Lathyrus "Sweet pea" *Leguminosae* 110+ species.   Eurasia, North America, temperate South Amercia. Named by the ancient Greeks, from *la*, addition; *thouros*, irritant. The seeds are said to rouse excitement. Some authorities mention aphrodisiac qualities.

Lavandula "Lavender" *Labiatae* 28 species.   Mediterranean, northern tropical Africa, west Asia, Arabia, India. Dictionaries seem uncertain of this word, though in the fourteenth century a lavender was a washerwoman, and even earlier it was a washerman. (C13)

Lilium "Lily" *Liliaceae* c.100 species.   Temperate northern hemisphere. Latin *lilium*. Related to the Greek *leirion*, lily.

Limonium "Sea lavender" "Statice" *Plumbaginaceae* c.150 species. Cosmopolitan. From Greek *leimōn*, meadow. Salt meadows are a common habitat. A certain deposit in bogs is called leimonite.

Luculia *Rubiaceae* c.5 species. East Asia. From *luculi swa*, a native name.

Malva *Malvaceae* 30 species.   Europe, Asia, South Africa. Latin name for mallow, used by Cicero, but finally from Greek *malakos*, softening, from its emollient qualities. See Althaea page 42. (C17)

Nandina "Heavenly bamboo" *Berberidaceae* 1 species.   India to Japan. Latinised from the Japanese name, *nandin*.

Nemesia *Scrophulariaceae* c.65 species. South Africa. Borrowed from Greek *nemesion*, a similar plant.

Nerium "Oleander" *Apocynaceae* 1 species.   Mediterranean to west China. From *neros*, moist, because of its preferred habitat.

Papaver "Poppy" *Papaveraceae* 50 species. Eurasia, Australia, South Africa, North America. From Latin *papaver*, poppy, derived from *pappa*, food or milk, an allusion to the milky latex. Latin's *pappa* is derived ultimately from baby language.

Sophora "Japanese pagoda tree" "New Zealand kowhai" *Leguminosae* 52 species.   Cosmopolitan. From Arabic *sophera*, a tree with pea-like flowers.

Sparaxis *Iridaceae* 6 species. South Africa. From *sparasso*, laceration, referring to the lacerated bracts.

Tamarix "Tamarisk" "Salt cedar" *Tamaricaceae* 54 species. West Europe and the Mediterranean to Asia, India. Latin, *tamarix*. (C15)

Thalictrum "Meadow rue" *Ranunculaceae* 130 species.   Greek, *thallo*, to grow green, with reference to the bright green shoots.

Verbascum "Mullein" *Scrophulariaceae* 250–300 species. Europe and Asia. Pliny named mullein *verbascum*, bearded. See the bearded stamens.

Verbena *Verbenaceae* 250 species. Tropical and subtropical America. For the Romans *verbena* was a sacred bough used in ceremony.

Viburnum "Wayfaring tree" *Caprifoliaceae* 150 or more species. Temperate northern hemisphere. Latin, *viburnum*, wayfaring tree. It's said to be common in hedges. (C18)

Index

Limonium 48
Linum 24
Liriodendron 10
Lisianthus 4
Lithops 36
Luculia 48
Lunaria 31
Lupinus 27
Lychnis 44

Malva 49
Mammillaria 37
Meconopsis 36
Melianthus 5
Mesembryanthemum 5
Mimosa 43
Monstera 21
Myosotidium 28
Myosotis 28

Nandina 49
Nemesia 49
Nephrolepsis 37
Nerium 49
Nigella 16
Odontoglossum 36
Omphalodes 37
Onosma 27
Onopordum 27
Orchis 38

Ornithogalum 27
Osmanthus 5
Osteospermum 8

Papaver 49
Passiflora 21
Pelargonium 26
Penstemon 12
Philodendron 11
Phlox 32
Phormium 45
Photinia 43
Physalis 37
Pittosporum 9
Plectranthus 5
Plumbago 41
Podocarpus 13
Portulaca 44
Primula 43
Pteris 38
Pyracantha 32
Ranunculus 26
Reseda 41
Rhododendron 3
Rhus 14
Rose 2
Rosmarinus 32

Salpiglossis 36
Salvia 41

Saponaria 41
Saxifraga 41
Scabiosa 40
Schizanthus 5
Scrophularia 40
Sedum 45
Sempervivum 19
Senecio 18
Solanum 44
Solidago 40
Sophora 49
Sparaxis 49
Stephanotis 21
Streptocarpus 13

Tamarix 49
Telopea 44
Thalictrum 49
Trifolium 12
Tropaeolum 22
Tulipa 25

Verbascum 49
Verbena 49
Viburnum 49
Vinca 44
Viola 15

Bibliography

The New Royal Horticultural Society, *Dictionary of Gardening* 1992
Reader's Digest Encyclopaedia of Garden Plants and Flowers
Concise Oxford Dictionary
Shorter Oxford Dictionary
Hutchinson's New 20th Century Encyclopaedia
Encyclopaedia of New Zealand
Collins English Dictionary
Stanley J. Palmer, *Palmer's Manual of Trees, Shrubs and Climbers*
Chambers Twentieth Century Dictionary
Concise Oxford Dictionary of Etymology
Charlton T. Lewis Ph.D., *Latin for Schools*
C. Chicheley Plowden, A *Manual of Plant Names*, 3rd edition, Allen & Unwin

FAY CLAYTON has had a life-long interest in gardening, but love of words has been predominant. Why *do* we give that flower that name? In the writing of these three books she found wide travel in the area of the Mediterranean, Scandinavia and in the three Americas – North, Central and South – to be a wonderful backdrop to research. She has in the last decade contributed columns on word origins to the *Christchurch Press*, the *Evening Post* and the *Dominion*, and has lectured extensively to botanical and other interested groups. By invitation, she is a member of the World Literary Academy since 1981.

RAYMOND MOLE was curator of the Otari Botanic Garden in Wellington from 1962, and, from 1967 was also curator of the Wellington Botanic Garden, until his retirement in 1991. He wrote many articles for horticultural journals and the press, on native and exotic plants. He was awarded the Loder cup for his outstanding contributions to the preservation and cultivation of the New Zealand flora.

JOHN DAWSON was Associate Professor and Chairperson of Botany at his retirement from Victoria University in 1988. He has published many articles, and since his retirement, several books on various aspects of New Zealand and New Caledonian plants and their communities.

PHILLIP HART, ex-pupil of Wainuiomata College and now in management, has illustrated the first two books in this trilogy and most of this one.

This Trilogy covers in all three hundred and forty-three garden plants and ornamentals. A complete bibliography is presented below.

The New Royal Horticultural Society, *Dictionary of Gardening*, 1992
Reader's Digest Encyclopaedia of Garden Plants and Flowers
Stanley J. Palmer, *Palmer's Manual of Trees, Shrubs and Climbers*
C. Chicheley Plowden, *A Manual of Plant Names*, Allen and Unwin
Alice M. Coates, *The Quest for Plants. A History of the Horticultural Explorers*
D. J. Mabberley, *The Plant Book*
The Complete Book of Herbs and Spices, Loewenfeld and Back, Reed Publishing
     Company
Concise Oxford Dictionary
Concise Oxford Dictionary of Etymology
Shorter Oxford Dictionary
Collins English Dictionary
Chambers Twentieth Century Dictionary
Hutchinson's New 20th Century Dictionary
Reader's Digest Great Illustrated Dictionary
Random House Dictionary, Unabridged
Concise Encyclopaedia of Greek and Roman Mythology, Collins
Latin for Schools, Charlton T. Lewis, Ph.D.
Our Living Language, Margaret Johnston, Whitcoulls
Encyclopaedia of New Zealand